FOREWORD

I have been a student of hospitality since working my first job at a family-owned Italian bakery in upstate New York. I've loved the industry ever since, working my way from the School of Hotel Administration at Cornell University to Chicago, where I built my career in sales at a boutique hotel before moving on to two, full-service catering companies. Now I own my own consulting business. Through all my experiences, I have continuously educated myself to stay creative and relevant in this ever-changing industry. But updated, written instructional resources are quite limited in our marketplace. Catering Chronicles is my solution. In these books, I hope to share my insight and passion with every employee, leader, manager, and owner, offering solutions on hot topics affecting the hospitality industry today.

Jennifer Perna

FOREWORD

Producing special events has been in my blood since the late 1980's, when I helped with underground raves in Los Angeles. Who knew how far I would come in the industry? By applying business techniques that I was learning in college, I could throw parties for a living. Through my undergrad and graduate programs at San Diego State University, I found I loved creating systems and running the operational, financial, and technical side of this fun industry. After 20 plus years and more than 10,000 events, a family move to New Orleans allowed me to set up a management consulting business and give back to the industry that gave so much to me. Catering Chronicles has lived in my head as an animated film for the last 10 years, and I'm glad I finally found a way to get those thoughts and ideas on to paper. I hope you can take one idea and make one change with each volume. Enjoy and keep working on those systems!

Francisco "Frank" Christian

We developed Catering Chronicles to be used as a series or a single volume to aid in training and education for students, owners and companies of all sizes.

Play Nice!

No More Sales vs. Service

Francisco Christian

Jennifer Perna

Editor - Elizabeth Heaton

Illustrator - Andy Andersen

ISBN 978-1-7368658-2-8

www.cateringchronicles.com

Play Nice! Table of Contents

Catering Chronicles

SALES:

This is purely a guess, but I would bet I've hired at least 100 sales consultants and event producers or sales assistants in my career. If I hired that many, I interviewed well over 300 candidates to get that result. As I honed my management and leadership skills, several things became more natural and easier to do--even enjoyable! For example, I could meet a candidate and know in the first five minutes if they had it in them to be a future sales star. I looked for grit, hustle, happiness, and the ability to hold a conversation.

I also learned that my best hires always had one key element on their resume: *experience working on the service side of our industry.* They had worked many a Saturday night when the rest of the world was enjoying their day off. They understood the nuts and bolts of our business, got their hands dirty, and had no qualms jumping in when needed.

After a few years, I actually started working in tandem with the director of service staffing to recruit for my open sales team positions. Without a doubt, my most qualified candidates came directly from the service team. They understood off-premise catering, they knew our multitude of venues, and they already were rooted in our company culture. I could often offer a full-time position to those who started working part-time to get their foot in the door. On the flip side, when I met a candidate who wasn't quite ready for sales but was a good candidate for our company, I always referred them over to the service team to start in a waitstaff position. There is no better way to learn whether or not this business is really for you than rotating through all offsite positions.

Some of my highest revenue sales people started in service. They were hands down the best closers with our customers. They created a level of comfort through their knowledge and experience, and they could effectively sell both the front and back of the house. It was one of my greatest joys as a mentor and coach to see their professional development when they realized that all the time and effort, they put into developing their core service skills paid off in making them better at their careers.

OPERATIONS:

At one point, our company had 100 full-time and 500 part-time and seasonal employees. As you can imagine, trying to instill our company vision for an event in each employee was tough. As a part-time employee who rose through the ranks to company president, I can say the most valuable training was when sales worked side-by-side with hourly employees. There is a camaraderie and quirkiness to the way events come together onsite through the team; the onsite event employees have a unique culture all their own. Our staffing manager was sales liaison, trainer, on boarder, change agent, conflict resolver, disciplinarian, and listener, all at the same time. The sales team needs to embrace this culture by cross training with back of house employees.

As an event supervisor or captain, having a salesperson there at the correct time makes all the difference for a smoother event. For one particular event, we had four floors, twelve stations, eight bars, passed welcome drinks, and multiple vendors to coordinate in less than two hours. The sales team sent the captains the event proposal with all the production notes ahead of time. Once the three trucks arrived onsite, the sales person was waiting to review the setup maps and timeline, and answer any questions. As the first of 40 staff members began to arrive, the sales person took a back seat and let the captains do their job. This is where the ballet of the special event industry takes place. This seamless choreography by all team members makes the experience great each and every time. In the famous words of Hannibal from the A-Team - *"I love it when a plan comes together!"*

Understanding the Value of Service & How to Sell It

Most caterers start their businesses because they have a passion for creating delicious food and designing beautiful events. As they continue to book larger and more frequent events, caterers need to expand their service team resources to accommodate this increased business. Quite often, this service piece is not strategically planned from the beginning but rather learned through necessity.

As off-premise caterers, the quality of our service teams, both front and back of house, is what truly differentiates us from our competition. Proactively developing your service team, including recruiting, training, providing ample work with timely paychecks, and retaining and retraining staff, may cost money, but is well worth the investment.

When defining the service team, we are generally referring to the various positions required for a successful off-premise event, including:

Front of House:

Management: Captain/Supervisor

Food Service: Waiters/Servers/Beverage Servers/Buffet Attendants/Clearers

Beverage Service: Bartenders/Beverage Captains/Bar Backs

Back of House:

Management: Lead Chef

Food Service: Hot & Cold Food Cooks/Hors D'Oeuvres Prep/Carving Station Attendants

Pantry: Porter/Dish Room/Truck

Sales teams often struggle to explain the price of service to customers when they do not fully understand or agree with the costs themselves. Teaching the sales team why service is the most important element of the event and how to sell this commodity to their customers will make your company unique.

Basic Sales and Service 101

The sales team is responsible for budgeting service team pricing during the proposal writing process, usually months prior to the actual event. It is their job to ask the customer questions during the proposal writing stage in order to properly quote project costs while maintaining the company's minimum standards for service. Each sales team member must understand several variables when building this budget, including:

1.   Style of Service

This includes seated/plated dinner service, buffet stations or full, seated buffet dining, passed hors d'oeuvres receptions, picnics, and family style dinners.

2.   Guest Count

The guest count is based on the guaranteed number of attendees contracted by the customer. At times, this number may vary from what the actual guest count is at the event.

3.   Event Time

The event time is the contracted start and end time. This does not include the service team's setup and breakdown times.

4.   Floor Plan

The floor plan design is based on the number of floors, rooms, kitchens, bars, buffet tables, and seating tables at the event. All pieces of furniture and points of service in every physical location should be defined to determine service needs and assignments.

5.   Venue Requirements

Each off-premise venue has its own rules and regulations that must be followed, and they often require additional staff positions.

6.   Client History

Client history is a valuable resource to maintain and revisit when you have a repeat event. Having a better understanding of what the same client has done in the past allows for better decisions on the front end.

Ninety-nine-point nine percent of my sales portfolio includes selling to corporate clients, business customers who host full-service events in their office or another venue. The beauty of corporate clients is they often repeat events. When you collect corporate client history after the first event, you can produce a better second event because you understand the client's likes and dislikes, and their guests' eating and drinking habits. This also allows for better resource planning from the beginning, saving both the caterer and the client money. For example, if I know my client's guests consumed 20 bottles of red wine and no vodka at their annual holiday party, and we cater the same party next year with the same guest list, I know to tell the client the beer, wine, and soda package is a better option for them. This also allowed the warehouse operations team to pack less product on the truck, reducing labor time and potential theft and waste.

7.   Geographic Distance

Determining the location and distance of the event and factoring in transportation arrangements for staff arrival and departure.

8.   Guest Demographics

Guest demographics often determine additional or unusual staffing requirements. For example, the age of the guests can affect an event. If a customer is hosting an event for seniors ages 65 and older, an educated salesperson should propose more tables and chairs than the standard event seating recommendations. The salesperson should also suggest the best style of service, such as a plated dinner or passed hors d'oeuvres reception, with an appropriate floor plan layout.

What We Hear About Sales and Service Staff

In our experience these are the common complaints, misconceptions, and statements from sales and service teams.

1.

Sales: Customers are not used to paying an event staffing fee.

Customers have been trained since they started dining out as kids that they pay for four things: food, beverage, tax, and a 15 to 20 percent tip. If we think about the waitstaff's salary at all, we assume it is included in the price of the food and beverage being served. Smart restaurateurs know to incorporate the cost of service into their food and beverage prices.

Caterers typically charge customers for food, beverage, tax, and an event staffing fee. Service tips, recommended but not required, are based on the customer's discretion.

We have created a new, unfamiliar price line for customers with the event staffing fee, making the customer feel like they're paying more for something that should already be included. Mind you, our food prices are significantly lower than restaurants' because we break out the pricing, but customers ignore that during contract negotiations. Although caterers are more transparent in their pricing, they fail to communicate and educate the customer about this difference. More often than not, this creates more apprehension than appreciation for the information.

Salespeople have to take the time during the initial client call to really understand their customers and how they will buy. This can be accomplished three ways:

Explain Your Pricing Structure

It is important to explain how you break out you're pricing the first time you work with a new customer. Remember, they are new to your proposal structure and new to your business. If they are a corporate client, they are most likely a more seasoned purchaser. If they are a social client, like a bride and groom or someone hosting a party in their home, this may be the one and only time they invest in something of this magnitude. It is important to let them know you break everything out in detail vs. bundling all pricing into the food and beverage price. That will help them understand your complete price.

Ask Who You Are Competing Against

Understanding who you are bidding against is imperative. When you know how your competitors propose their pricing, you can better explain variances in your own pricing model. How do you accomplish this? Shop for proposals. Review their websites. Ask for a copy of your competition's proposal so you can compare line by line. If a customer is hesitant to share others' proposals, ask your customer to share your proposal with the competitor. (Remember one thing: once you send out a document, it is *public.* Do not get hung up on this. The more information you can gather for your own knowledge base, the better.)

Modify Your Pricing Page to Meet Customer Preferences

Ask your customer if they want a complete breakout or if they prefer a more streamlined pricing page. If you are using a catering system, you most likely can bundle the pricing internally without affecting cost centers. You then can show the catering investment on a customized pricing proposal page based on you customer's request.

Service: **Sales didn't sell enough staff for this event.**

Staff usually gets 45 minutes to an hour to look over their paperwork or supervisor board before the truck leaves for the event location. The staff doesn't really understand how much still needs to be set up until they arrive onsite, unload the truck, and assess the actual physical space. Sales tried to meet the client budget, and used history and formulas to gauge staff onsite time. But there is never a way to factor real life into the timing of event setup. To help with this challenge, the captain, event supervisor, or chef needs to fully complete the evaluation form at the end of each event. The more knowledge captured that day, the better the next event will be.

When sales put the event together, that initial staff request to the staffing coordinator is based on everything going exactly as initially proposed. As the event evolves and the client makes changes, budget increases often do not include staff changes. By failing to incorporate staffing changes alongside event changes, the sales team may inadvertently create time crunches the day of the event. During production and post-production meetings, make the staffing coordinator aware of event changes so that they can consider additional staff and onsite needs. Most of the time, the client can be charged for additional staff, but the catering company may sometimes absorb the expense for the benefit of the event.

2.

Sales: **Front of house staff just stands around.**

Salespeople are often challenged when they see the front of house staff standing around during both the event setup and the event itself.

There are so many variables that make every event setup different. The service captain may be efficient and organized in managing their team. The event may be scheduled with the A team of regular staff members. On the flip side, the freight elevator may break down during load in or the company may be so busy that 50 percent of the team may come from a staffing rental agency.

It is the service captain's job to keep the front of house active and on task. It is also the salesperson's job to schedule all events with the recommended staffing ratios provided by service leadership. These staffing ratios should be developed based on the logic of typical busy days throughout the year along with the available pool of staff. They should also include a time buffer for any situation that may arise

Service: **We like working Sally Salesperson's events because she always sells more setup and tear-down time than we need.**

Any experienced salesperson knows that selling extra staff time for setup and tear-down is necessary for a successful event. Sally sells not only the company but her expertise in solving the client's pain points. Because she has years and years of event experience, service teams like working for Sally Salesperson. She makes sure there is ample time to calmly set up an event. If you are new to the business and to selling, you often question whether or not you *really* need that extra staff person two hours before the event. You will try anything to get the sale, and often look at service as an area to cut. Don't do it! Be like Sally Salesperson and trust the data and staffing models your company has developed. They are based on years of experience.

3.

Sales: **Staff costs too much already.**

Sales people always want the best service team to work their events. But getting the best service team costs money. This is common sense: you get what you pay for. If the company wants to be competitive in recruiting highly talented people, they need to offer an enticing hourly wage. This in turn needs to be marked up at appropriate margins to achieve company profitability targets.

When presenting the staffing fees to their customers, sales people can explain that they offer a competitive wage to provide for training, recruiting, and maintaining a high-quality staff. "We always guarantee the A team on your event."

Service: **Company XYZ pays more but they don't do enough events for me to make enough money working for them.**

Part-time or seasonal staff are much different than full time staff. Staff cannot make money waiting for the phone to ring, which means they may be on call for multiple companies. Experienced salespeople understand this and often give the staff manager a heads up on future events they are working on. This helps to fill the staff's calendar within your company. The more you communicate with your event staff, the more available they will be for your company. The more events your company does each week, month, and year, the more reliable your staff will be. They know they can count on your company for work, and they will reward you with their loyalty.

4.

Sales: **Our staff turnover is too high.**

The seasonality of the catering business is a big reason why it is difficult to retain a consistent service team. Depending on your geographic region, there are frequent months with minimal business, or no business at all. For example, in Chicago, January through March is an extremely slow period, while you can say the same for July through August in Phoenix. It is common for team members to leave after peak season to find new jobs at stable, year-round hospitality operations.

Large event caterers also struggle with staff retainment. They may have one huge event that requires massive hiring, only to not need these staff members again until the next large event. It is important for sales professionals to consider this when managing the company event calendar, including driving promotional sales efforts. If it's possible to recommend better pricing or higher value events to customers in slower seasons, this can spread out the event calendar and provide more work for your service team.

Service: Most staff are not looking for full time work.

Only about 25 percent of your pool of part-time or seasonal employees will want to work full-time. For some staff, working events provide supplemental or play money, while others depend on this income as their primary means of support. Regardless of their goals in doing this work, your staff needs to understand when they can expect to get work with your company. During the hiring process, the staffing coordinator should be very clear about the times of the year when they need staff. Without clear expectations about when they will be needed next, staff will make other plans. Be sure to have hiring parameters in place so there is no ambiguity.

5.

Sales: Both clients and salespeople only want certain service team members to work their events.

Salespeople need to let this go. I am sure there are certain service team members who *do not* want to work your events or for some specific clients. Salespeople need to let that go too. It is the staffing coordinator's job to assign each service team employee to each event, and many things need to be considered when juggling multiple events, team availability, and salespeople's wants.

It is understandable when customers, especially for home events, get comfortable with certain people. Service team members often become like part of the customer's family. It is perfectly fine to ask for specific team members based on client requests, but never guarantee it. When possible, spread the wealth and introduce your clients to more members of your team. Invest the extra money and send a second team member to shadow and work the event to get to know the client as well.

Rather than limiting your opinions of specific team members, broaden your service pool. Get to know all your service team members. I guarantee that on peak service days, you will be happy with any team member representing you at an event. If a service team member has the confidence of their own managers, you must follow.

Service: I try to work other event coordinator's events but those seem to quickly fill up.

Time and time again, salespeople get so used to a staffing team that they request them all the time. When business is slow, it's great to have all of the A team. But if you want your company to grow, you must be willing to staff with a mix of A and B team members, and let the A team train the B team. Sales needs to trust the staff development process to sell out days in the future. The A team can only be stretched so far, and as a company grows, so should the staffing department.

6.

Sales: We should do more advanced culinary production work at the shop.

The company's philosophy on food production is important here. Just as important is the production facility. Depending on the food sold, sometimes it *is* more effective to produce more food at the shop; sometimes it is better to finish the food on site for the best quality.

There are some steps the sales team can take to alleviate the workload at the event, including using the rental vendor's support teams to set up tables and chairs, linens, and other items. Having an organized timeline and flowchart of deliveries and set up will ease this typically tight time prior to the event.

Service: If sales doesn't want us to interpret the recipes, do more in the kitchen.

Kitchen versus onsite chefs will always be a battle. Kitchen staff thinks the onsite culinary team needs their hands held, while the onsite team always thinks the kitchen staff could do more. The best way to train through this problem is to use your onsite staff in the kitchen one or two days a week during your busy times of the year rather than hiring kitchen temps. Conversely, every great catering operation routinely sends their kitchen staff into the field. By allowing staff to see and better understand both sides of the food production process, sales will feel comfortable selling the most profitable recipes.

7.

Sales: Other caterers don't require as much of their onsite service team members.

You never really know what other caterers promise their staff members. Although your onsite work requirements may be different, you may provide benefits that your competitors do not. Perhaps you offer a higher hourly rate, more hours per month, or more organized events. This is a conversation the sales team should stay out of; focus on providing work opportunities through proactive selling.

Service: The culture of this company is great. I would run through a wall for them.

All staff stay or leave a company because of the culture and its people. You may have the best onsite staff, but if sales make the timing of an event difficult, your staff pool will be doomed. Sales needs to embrace the onsite staff as the ultimate line of defense for a successful event. Some event coordinators always show up on site with treats, coffee, or Red Bulls. That goes a long way. Salespeople who are onsite when the truck arrives, help coordinate the initial unload, stay until the end to make sure the client is happy, or say please and thank you when stress levels are high, will usually have the most loyal staff pools.

8.

Sales: **This is just a part-time job for our service team so they don't need to care.**

This cannot be a global statement. Service team members work in the hospitality industry for a variety of reasons. What is important is that when a service team member is on the clock, they are representing your brand. Let part-timers know there are future job opportunities for career growth if they so desire.

Service: **Going from part time to a service team leader is hard.**

If the staffing coordinator has done a good job during the hiring and onboarding process, the company will know which staff is willing to work full-time hours when the business dictates. Those staff willing to work full-time are usually the ones who seek out training and opportunities with the company. They will also like to see that there is a growth path in the organization.

This is another reason why sales should not repeatedly request the same staff. The more staff positions an employee can learn, the more availability and value they will have to the company. Staff looking to work full time will take any shifts they are qualified for to keep building their hours. Let your staff check the box on as many skill types as they are willing to learn. A good pool of staff cannot have enough good team leaders in training.

9.

Sales: **Rental staff is never good.**

As a catering company grows in size, their staffing needs expand, and they may need to outsource staffing on peak event dates. To maximize success, it is important to effectively research staffing companies. Following is a list of questions to consider when shopping for a rental company:

What are you looking for and do they represent your brand?

Who do your competitors use?

Will they invest in in-office service training based on your company standards?

Will they have their own leadership or ownership onsite at large events?

Once you decide on your rental staff partners, make sure you invest a little extra time prior to the event to teach rental staff members a bit about your company. Not only do you want to make sure these staff members represent your company and brand, you want them to actually know who they are working for in case a guest asks for a referral.

Service: **As your staff vendor, we never get enough information before the event.**

Your temporary staff company should be treated as an ally and not a thorn in your side. There are times when the temporary staff does not meet sales expectations, but if there is a good working relationship with the company, you may be able to get a timely replacement. Sales should provide the staff coordinator with as much advance information as possible as early as possible. The staff company is in a similar position to a catering company; when it rains it pours. The more information the company has on the future, the better prepared the temporary staff company will be to help you.

10.

Sales: Sales doesn't have confidence in the service team if mistakes continue to happen.

Salespeople never forget. One mistake by the service team can ruin an event and a customer relationship. If something negative happens, it is imperative that the salesperson be immediately notified so they can check in with the customer to make sure they are okay. It is also important for the service team leader to be part of the solution if they want the customer to stick with the company for future events. This shows the sales team that service has their back. Mistakes will happen--we are human. The key is learning from past mistakes and taking steps to prevent them from happening again.

Service: Sales need more onsite training. The staff only sees them for a few minutes at events.

Event staff can be very helpful trainers when onboarding new sales team members. Sales should visit more than just their team or division events. By seeing multiple events in different stages of production, sales team members will grow in their event knowledge. The more knowledge a sales team member has, the better they are as a trusted advisor for the client. The most successful companies have a training onboarding program that includes a checklist with event set up, tear down, and ride alongs. Peer training in the hospitality industry is the greatest knowledge management system.

11.

Sales: **Our venue representatives only want specific team members to work at their space**

A forward-thinking sales and business development strategy provides staffing team consistency at your top non-exclusive venues, including designating specific event captains as leads at these venues. Venue representatives should be seen as an extension of your own organization; they are our collaborative partners. If you make them more comfortable with consistent staffing, it is more likely that they will recommend future clients to you as a preferred caterer. This helps support the sales team efforts in maintaining strong venue relationships.

Service: **As a staff member, I wish I could work at more venues to be more well-rounded.**

As a great partner to your venues, your catering company should hire as many of your staff pool as possible throughout all your venues. This allows for last minute bookings, staff changes due to emergencies, and staff management during busy times of the year. Your sales team and venue should feel comfortable with any members of your staff. Part of your part-time and seasonal training and onboarding program should include a rotational shift at all exclusive and preferred venues. Your staffing coordinator should have a venue training checklist in each staff member's file and staff their shifts accordingly.

Next Steps: Actionable Change List: Six Steps Sales Managers Should Take Today

In order to change the sales team's mindset, encourage them to appreciate the service team's efforts, and actively sell high-quality service, we recommend these steps:

1.   Develop Educational Programming.

Creating opportunities to educate the team throughout the year allows for continuous improvement and cross-department appreciation. By training and retraining on a consistent basis, sales managers can revisit recurring sales and service challenges while newly hired employees can learn about these issues. Following are three examples of establishing educational programming:

Sales Meetings

Invite service team leaders to attend sales meetings on a monthly basis to discuss service team updates, introduce new salaried hires, and review the upcoming event calendar for hot dates. Create a meeting agenda in advance and allot time for this conversation. Let the service team managers lead the session.

Service Team Meetings

Inviting the director of sales to quarterly or semiannual service team meetings allows this team to hear updates on sales team efforts. Examples of updates to share include customer feedback, revenue numbers, tasting close rates, and new sales team hires.

Service Team Training Sessions

Involve salespeople in the initial service team training sessions so the sales team can see service leadership's efforts to provide consistent, high-quality service. This may involve participating in an actual training session or performing in hands-on training videos.

2.   Ask for Customer Feedback

Asking different customers for feedback on service quality can provide valuable information for all departments. It is important to curate a group of customers with a broad range of event types, service styles, guest counts, and venue locations. It is also important to collect information from both new and experienced customers who have been loyal to your services for many years. You can gather this information in a few different ways, including online surveys, focus groups, telephone conversations, or in-person meeting reviews. Additional considerations for feedback include your off-premise venue representatives. Do not forget your drop-off customers in the feedback process. Service does not only mean front of house in this scenario; a delivery driver is considered the service provider when dropping off food.

3.   Define Sales Consultants' Purpose at Events

It is imperative that company leadership define the management "ownership" piece of each offsite event. From a management perspective, defining whether the back or front of house runs the event is an extremely important detail when it comes to organizational structure and processes. From a cultural perspective, it speaks volumes regarding off site communication and perceptions.

Depending on the size of your company, it is strongly recommended that service and culinary, in this case collectively defined as back of house, run all offsite events. They are the core of your operation and make the events happen. In theory, the salesperson releases all ownership of the event once production paperwork is released to these teams. Hence, they should also release all event management duties.

Early in a salesperson's career, It is important to learn the ropes by working events so they understand every facet of the product they are selling. Eventually though, a salesperson's role at the event should be to support the customer and act as liaison between customers and service. A pass off to the event supervisor or captain must happen. Imagine if the event supervisor or captain is introduced to the customer at the beginning of the event during setup, rather than when the cake is being cut? That is a much more desirable timeframe for a proper introduction between the parties.

Remember: from the beginning, the salesperson is touting your company's high-level of service, and the need to detail and bill for all positions. If a customer sees a salesperson running an event, then what are they paying for with that event staffing fee line? Was the event captain an extraneous position? Of course not. *We* know that behind the scenes, but what are they seeing?

Salespeople need to be salespeople. Ideally, they should keep their car running so they can run in, kiss the client, and move on to visiting the second of four events booked that evening. Let the service team run the show.

4.   Onboard Sales People Through All Service Positions

Developing a cross-departmental onboarding process for newly hired sales employees provides a solid foundation and appreciation for all company team members. With a particular focus on the service department, the sales hire should work through every position in the field prior to working in the office. The director of sales should collaborate with the staffing coordinator to develop the onboarding schedule. They should review the event calendar and select a wide range of events based on size, location, type, and available position. It is also important to work on various salespeople's events so the new hire can see different styles and approaches. The staffing coordinator should give the director of sales a report on the new hire's progress and determine when the onboarding program is complete.

5.   Effective Customer Event Planning

When developing the customer proposal during the buying process, the salesperson should review the criteria discussed when they created the sales estimate (see section one). One further step to ensure service and sales collaboration is requesting service team leadership for assistance on more complicated, detailed proposals. Asking for this input in advance allows for a more strategic approach to proposal development as well as the obvious benefit of collaborative teamwork.

6.   Produce Timely Service Team Staffing Requests

Sales team members should be respectful of the service team's time and send in staff requests using common sense. This will allow them to book better quality staff in advance and hold rental staff if needed. The following scenarios should be considered:

- If the event is going to go to contract, send the staffing request in immediately
- If the event is a larger than a normal event, let the service team know about it during the proposal stage
- If the event is during peak season, ask staff if service team is still available, and if it is okay to propose
- If the event guest count changes, let the service team know immediately about the increased or decreased needs
- If the event style or location changes, let the service team know immediately so they can make adjustments

One last consideration: support the service team during the event. If the guest count increases well beyond the guaranteed count, and staff needs to work longer hours or beyond the normal scope of their position, discuss the guest count increase with the customer at the event and let them know there will be additional charges. This typically does not affect food volume but does make an impact on beverage, disposables, equipment rental, and other items, and the client should be appropriately charged. Letting the service team know you have their back is important so they can take care of the employees who put in the extra effort.

See you in the next Catering Chronicle...

VOL. 2

FULTON MARKET

Catering Chronicles

MAKE MORE MONEY

BUDGETING AS YOUR FIRST STEP

FRANCISCO CHRISTIAN
JENNIFER PERNA

Make More Money!

Budgeting As Your First Step

Francisco Christian

Jennifer Perna

Editor - Elizabeth Heaton

Illustrator - Andy Andersen

www.cateringchronicles.com

This information is based on our decades of experience in the industry. Please consult your CPA or attorney if you have any questions related to the rules and regulations in your particular state.

Make More Money! Table of Contents

Catering Chronicles

You cannot run a successful catering business without a budget. Period. Market conditions during this new economic rebound will be unlike any others in the past. As the industry reopens and owners manage cash flow every day, recovery and budgeting needs to be a focus. Companies that run their business without a budget will not have the vision to react to revenue fluctuations. Now is the time to reset your company with an overall budget.

OPERATIONS:

Sharing budget information with employees is a scary endeavor, but this practice is valuable to a company's success. When I became warehouse manager, I had four budget line-item responsibilities--vehicle maintenance, equipment maintenance, building maintenance, and fuel costs-- out of 20. My team and I focused on keeping within budget no matter what wild, unexpected expenses popped up, like having to repair the roof of a catering truck that somehow got stuck in the drive through of a Wienersnitzel. Once I was promoted to director of operations, I had access and responsibility for all the budget line items. I was now overseeing accounting, IT administration, culinary, staffing, and the warehouse. Because of my finance background, could help the other managers understand how their budgeting decisions should be based on sales goals rather than their personal projects.

Our company used the Great Game of Business, developed by Jack Stack, to educate all employees, including our 400-part time and seasonal staff, on basic financial literacy. We trained them to understand that throwing away an extra 10 or 15 plastic utensils was real cash money we could never recover. At the end of the year, employees understood that raises, bonuses, or year-end parties could be affected if our disposable cost line item was over budget.

From an operational perspective, budgeting is all about managing costs. Sales comes up with their goals, and the company's remaining departments have to try not to spend all of the gross profit. There is always a need for new equipment, vehicle repairs, and building maintenance; the expenses go on and on. But once your managers understand that staying in business means hanging on to your net income, the game of building and sustaining a viable business takes over.

Starting out and creating an annual budget seems like a major rock to push up a hill, and, possibly as a result, the number of businesses that Jennifer and I work with that don't do budgets is staggering. But just like eating an elephant, it's one bite at a time. Once budgeting becomes part of your business' annual plan, you can look at department incentives and bonuses based on cost savings. As managers learn to adjust their budgets and spend to the sales revenue peaks and valleys of the industry, your company becomes stronger. By reviewing the monthly increased profitability, your company can make growth decisions, acquisitions, and partnerships by comparing how the increased revenue will impact your bottom line. Without taking that first giant budgeting leap, you can never acquire competitors, expand into new lines of business, or know when your cash flow will be tight.

SALES:

I worked at two independently owned companies during my catering career. One owner was private and only worked with the in-house accountant on the budget and yearly profitability goals. The other was an open book, inviting the leadership team to participate in the annual revenue and expense planning process. As a leader in both organizations, can definitively state that I was more effective in making short and long-term sales decisions at the second company. I appreciated learning *how* we as a company made money and understanding what was a good sale and what was not. I could then teach my team the same principles, which made them smarter sales people for both the organization and their clients.

For example, I learned very quickly that food and beverage were the two largest profit centers within the sale, as these two areas traditionally have the highest markups. This is obvious to back of house operators and owners because they live and breathe costs and expenses. But front of house thinkers live and breathe revenue: *we do not think about costs unless we are introduced to them.* Once I learned this, I always put the biggest emphasis on this part of the sale in my sales mix. If a customer had 100 dollars to spend, I always wanted to grab the biggest piece of that 100-dollar pie with food and beverage. didn't want the customer to spend as much money on entertainment, linens, and tents when I could sell them an upgraded bar package and an extra dessert station. This meant more profit for our bottom line on items we were going to sell anyway.

This has to be taught to salespeople. As an owner, determine what methodology you are comfortable with. Then share and teach your team to better understand how to sell for a bigger profit. Once you invest the time to budget and develop event profitability goals, give your sales team ranges to sell within these goals. I guarantee you will see an increase in event profitability percentage points in your first year of introducing this new way of selling and thinking. I bet you see even higher than you aim for once the salespeople realize they can control how they sell the ratio of products and services for their events.

Budgeting 101 for Catering

Operations:

Catering is such a creative industry that we sometimes forget that the basics of running the business requires that we stay in business. Over the last 20 plus years, the number of business owners I have met who don't use a budget or put together an annual budget is astonishing. While some of these owners are still in business, others have shut their doors because they didn't know which day they would run out of money. Budgets are key to your managers participating in running your business. By empowering your staff to be mindful of expenses and how they impact your budget, their entrepreneurial spirit will help to find more efficient and cost-effective ways to get the job done.

When I start with new clients, the first questions I want to ask are about the financial health of the business. Is the company on track to hit their annual budget? Has the company had to re-budget midyear due to loss of business or adding a new revenue line? I am consistently surprised that companies don't create a map for their journey simply because the budgeting process is going to be too hard or they don't know where to start.

If a company has been in business for three or more years, the owner has everything they need to put together a yearly budget. By using the last three years as a starting point, look at the averages of revenue, costs, and expenses. This will take into account one-off, or anomaly events that happen every year. We define an anomaly event as a gift from the catering heavens, something not forecasted or budgeted, a lucky proposal won, or a once in a lifetime event.

While revenue is the most important piece of the budgeting puzzle, basic operating expenses help build the budget and tell the owner how much revenue they need in order to make a profit at the end of the year. We will discuss cash flow versus profit, but for now let's focus on net income in our budgeting process. While budgets seem like a major undertaking, the formula is pretty simple:

- Revenue - Direct and Event Costs = Gross Profit
- Gross Profit - Overhead and Expenses = Net Income

By working backwards and understanding what your monthly non-variable expenses are, your company budget will start to take shape. Examples of non-variable expenses include rent, utilities, technology, health care, and insurance. The next level of expenses should relate to the revenue or direct costs. The old saying, "there is no such thing as free lunch" is the same for revenue. Every $1 that comes into the company as revenue has some cost or expense. For example, if you sell an item for 20 dollars but the item costs you 10 dollars, then that item will have a direct cost of 50 percent. Once you establish the percentage of direct costs for a line-item cost category (food, labor, equipment rental, etc.) you can figure out your direct cost section of your budget.

Budgets can be scary, but they are very necessary. You need to know when there will be a cash crunch or when major payments are due. Your business may be seasonal, and, while there is a boom in revenue some months, those expenses stay the same during the lean months. Some businesses are fortunate and may have contracts or clients that run year-round. This is nice, but normally not the case in our industry. From an operations view point, budgets help the team understand when to start staffing up and when to contract. As we walk through some examples below, keep in mind that some type of budget visited multiple times a year is better than no budget at all.

Sales:

A sales leader's primary purpose is to drive revenue. They need to inspire their team to sell profitable events throughout the year. Yet quite often when a company does not have a road map on the front end to measure success, the sales team has no idea if they have had a good sales year or even sold profitable events. The first step to fix this is developing an annual budgeted revenue goal broker down into monthly targets. These revenue goals in turn allow all other departments, including sales, to create direct cost and overhead expense budgets based on these targeted numbers.

If your organization has historical revenue data, this process is typically easier than starting from scratch. Assuming you run on a calendar fiscal year, it is strongly recommended that sales leadership start next year's revenue goal setting process in August in order to have a revenue number by the end of the year. Why August? The numbers created in August go through many negotiations between sales team members, owners, and department heads before agreement, which means you need a five-month lead time. Each salesperson should develop their own annual sales goal and break out that goal into monthly targets. Once the monthly targets are added together, the annual sales goal should be in line with the company's history yet also allow for revenue growth based on leadership's guidance.

Below is a sample for Sally Salesperson, a seasoned salesperson who is setting an annual goal of $600,000 for calendar year 2021:

Salesperson Name: Sally Salesperson
Sales Plan Time Period: January 1 - December 31, 2021
Annual Sales Goal: $ 600,000
Monthly Target Breakouts within Annual Goal
January	$20,000
February	$25,000
March	$30,000

April	$50,000
May	$75,000
June	$75,000
July	$25,000
August	$25,000
September	$75,000
October	$75,000
November	$50,000
December.	$75,000

You may notice fluctuations in numbers throughout the year. Some examples for the rationale behind these varied numbers include catering's seasonality, repeatable events, and the catering company's location. If the company has no previous revenue history, we strongly recommend that the salesperson develop the sales goal based on logic, educated assumptions, and potential business development patterns built on the caterer's location, market segmentation, and business lines. It is extremely rare for a salesperson to create their annual goal by dividing the annual number by 12 to determine the monthly target. The catering industry is too seasonal and fluid for that approach.

Getting your Budget Done!

So where do you start? We will discuss some basic budget line items below to get you thinking about your own business. We know that your business is unique, so we have provided some basics to review in each category that you can tailor your budget to your situation.

Revenue

Sales - There are different scenarios for an established company and a new company. For companies that have been in business for three or more years, the last three years are the only ones that really matter.

Operations - The decision about what to charge should come from the operations departments setting their pricing for sales. Operations should give sales the profitable retail price for items or services once the details are passed along from sales. There should be an annual pricing calendar that the company agrees upon so all departments have time to gather new costs, labor, and any other factors that affect pricing.

Sample Revenue Line Items

Food Revenue
There are different approaches to what makes up food revenue, so determining your approach is an important business decision. Here are a few ways to look at food revenue:

Scenario 1:
- Food and Kitchen Labor Cost covered
- Food Product Direct Cost - $1.00
- Five times markup to kitchen labor, food costs and kitchen supplies - $5 retail
- Assumes a 20% food cost goal

Scenario 2:
- Software used to calculate retail pricing

- Costs of ingredients all entered into the software
- Example Food Cost % used - Ex. 23%
- This will also help to cover kitchen labor, food costs and kitchen supplies

Beverage Revenue

Depending on your state and the ability to have an Alcohol Beverage Control (ABC) license, you will break this down as:

- Soft Beverages
- Beer
- Wine
- Liquor

This is for insurance purposes and the proper revenue tracking for sales tax and any other related taxes on the sale of alcoholic beverages.

Staff Revenue

Yes, staff should be a profit center. Most profitable catering companies price their staff above the labor costs they actually pay. You should be taking into consideration the administrative time and costs to recruit, train, hire, process payroll, and keep records on staff for up to three years, more in some states.

Vendor and Third-Party Revenue

Entertainment

Typically, vendors of this sort are marked up based on the convenience of providing a one-stop shop for the customer. Typical markups range from 25 to 50 percent or even higher depending on the complexity of the event or service provided. As a general guideline, markup must be set in such a way as to produce a reasonable profit. Profit is the difference between revenue and the cost. For example, when you are invoiced 80 dollars for a service and sell it for 100 dollars, your profit is 20 dollars. The ratio of profit ($20) to cost ($80) is 25 percent, so 25 percent is the markup.

Please do not confuse margin and markup. In the example above, the margin is 20 percent, which is your 20-dollar profit. Often, we hear caterers talk about their margin, but they really mean the markup they are charging across a service category. There are many helpful margin and market calculators online that are free to use.
https://corporatefinanceinstitute.com/resources/templates/excel-modeling/markup-calculator-formula/
https://www.omnicalculator.com/finance/markup

Equipment Rentals
This can be either internal equipment that you rent to customers or costs you pass along to the customer for equipment from a rental company. If you choose not to keep sub-rentals separate as a revenue line item, keep in mind there might be a different profit percentage based on your own equipment versus rental equipment.

Linen Rentals
Since there is so much lost and damaged linen in our industry, keeping track of your linen revenue will help manage replacement linen costs. Some companies will own and maintain their own linen inventory and charge a damage waiver to offset replacement costs. Most rentals for glassware, china, flatware, and linen have a damage waiver line item

passed along to the customer. This damage waiver is used to replace or cover the cost for lost, stolen or damaged items. Damage waiver revenue should be a separate revenue line as well.

Room Rental
If you have an on premise or exclusive venue revenue line of business, it's good to include room rental fees as a revenue line to support building and event room maintenance.

Miscellaneous/Administrative Revenue

Delivery Fees
These are usually treated as a 100 percent cost item, but you want to know what you collected to offset vehicle insurance and maintenance.

Service Charge
Depending on your state regulations, you may be able to include a service charge, which the customer perceives as covering staff charges related to the event. While this may not be treated like a gratuity, most companies use this revenue pool to help pay a competitive wage in the market. Please check with your local tax commission to understand your state's specific rules.

Rush Charges
In the last few years, companies have been keeping track of and passing along to customers the last-minute change costs arising from late planning. The window from prospect call to event production in the catering industry has tightened two weeks on average. With that comes unexpected costs that the company should not eat. By keeping track of these

rush charges, the company may be able to figure out where the process is breaking down between the client and sales.

Administration Fees
With the increasing costs of insurance, workers compensation, and business licenses, this line item is now becoming more common in the catering industry. If a company tried to pass along these costs through food pricing, we would all be selling $10 hot dogs on picnic menus. The administration fee helps to cover the costs of the above-mentioned items plus client site walk throughs, proposal changes, calls to vendors, site map production, and other event-related tasks, and helps you remain competitive in your local market.

The more lines you break down on your proposal, the better the information you will have to determine all sources of revenue.

Direct Costs
Once you've established revenue goals, you need to apply your direct cost percentages to that revenue. We have provided a guide with industry averages, but your business may have higher or lower percentages depending on your market and your buying programs. Keep in mind that these percentages are related to the revenue categories discussed above. This is where the spreadsheet magic comes in handy. You can create easy formulas to give you a good look at how your overall gross profit changes based on revenue in a particular line of business.

Typical Industry Ranges:

- Warehouse Labor, Hourly Employees - 3 to 5%
- Kitchen Labor, Hourly Employees - 12 to 20%
- Event Labor, Hourly Employees - 50%
- Food Cost - 18 to 25%
- Soft Bev Cost - 50%
- Liquor - 35%
- Disposables - 1 to 3%
- Vendors - 35%
- Venues/Third Party Commissions - 10 to 15%
- Service Charge - 50 to 100%
- Payroll Taxes for Hourly Employees
- Workers Compensation for Hourly Employees

Expenses

- Rent - 10%
- Sales Expenses 1 to 2%
  - Meals & Entertainment
  - Transportation
  - Travel
  - Education
  - Dues and Subscriptions
  - Client Gifts
- Marketing Labor and Expenses - 1 to 3%
  - In-house and/or Outsourced Services
  - Advertising & Promotions
  - Open Houses
  - Sponsorships
  - Print Media
  - Social Media
- Salaries - 30 to 40%
  - Sales
  - Administrative

- Executive Chef
- Operations Director
- Finance IT and Accounting

The following line items do not have industry standards but are common to all companies:
- Employee Health
- Utilities/Telephone/Data Processing
- Building Maintenance
- Equipment Maintenance
- Vehicle Maintenance
- Gas/Mileage
- Human Resources/Training
- Uniforms
- Audit/Legal
- Property Taxes
- Bank Charges
- Interest Income/Expense
- Depreciation

Net Income/Loss

A company will manage this Net Income/Loss based on their long-term goals. Some companies like to show a 10 to 20 percent EBITDA (Earnings before Interest, Taxes and Depreciation) if they are looking to sell their business in three to five years. Other companies like to show a loss on paper but their cash flow might be great for the owners. Whatever your company strategy, your CPA and ownership group should be in alignment. Here is a helpful resource to answer some of your questions https://corporatefinanceinstitute.com/resources/knowledge/finance/what-is-ebitda/

See you in the next Catering Chronicle...

May We Join You?

Investing in Non-Exclusive Venue Relationships

Francisco Christian

Jennifer Perna

Editor - Elizabeth Heaton

Illustrator - Andy Andersen

www.cateringchronicles.com

This information is based on our decades of experience in the industry. Please consult your CPA or attorney if you have any questions related to the rules and regulations in your particular state.

May We Join You? Table of Contents

Catering Chronicles

SALES:

As a sales leader for most of my career, my relationship with off-premise venue representatives was the key to achieving revenue goals. I always invested significant time nurturing relationships with venue owners, managers, and internal sales teams. Although the end clients were our paying customers, and we took great care of them, venue representatives were equally important. They were customers 365 days a year.

Toward the end of my catering career, I managed a very large sales team with a stellar reputation in the Chicagoland region. Besides managing more than 30 sales team employees, I was also responsible for maintaining our team's high selling standards and practices at over 85 non-exclusive off-premise venues. Thankfully, in tandem with our vice president of business development, we tackled each venue with a high level of professionalism by pushing our team to be the best, most responsive, proactive sales team in the market. This also meant at times we had to make very important, challenging decisions in order to satisfy the venue's requirements and desires. These decisions were tough because our own sales team members did not always like the resulting changes.

Catering salespeople are accustomed to receiving most of their leads from the venue. This is so prevalent today that I often refer to salespeople as account managers. This also means the catering salesperson's compensation was often tied to "owning" specific venues and receiving their leads from the venue.

There are several factors in determining who is the best salesperson for each specific venue. For example, we always matched the appropriate sales team member with the lead on-site venue representative. This is a fundamental of sales and essential to creating strong relationships. People like to work with people they like, so I tried to match individuals with similar personalities and common interests. On the flip side, the venue may have requested a change. Perhaps the venue wanted a wedding-focused salesperson versus a convention-minded one. Or the venue rep may have seen better results with another of my salespeople. The venue may also have their own staffing change, which in turn made a different team member a better relationship fit.

Finally, every year I revisited the venue assignment list to compare our revenue totals to prior years. If I saw a reduction in revenue, I would ask the salesperson about their efforts to try to understand why the sales decreased. If there were minimal sales, business development and relationship building, I often made the decision to change the salesperson assigned to the venue.

The beauty of leading and managing a sales department is that there is always factual data to back up company-wide decisions. Making changes based on what was best for our non-exclusive venues was more important than hurting the feelings of an upset salesperson. If I didn't make the change, we could ultimately be removed from that venue list. Nobody wins in that situation.

OPERATIONS:

One of my favorite non-exclusive venues was the USS Midway Museum (Midway). A retired aircraft carrier docked in San Diego Bay, the Midway is one of the most unique venues in any city. In order to work there, catering companies had to audition and be selected as a preferred catering partner. At the time of audition, the Midway had not settled on their standard operating procedures. Instead, each company received the same load in parameters, and the Midway asked them to contribute a list of best practices that should be incorporated into producing their events.

Some of the unique challenges the Midway presented included:

- All food, beverage and equipment needed to be put on pallets so they could be loaded off the truck with a pallet jack or forklift.
- Once the pallets were offloaded, they had to be transferred to a converted open container to get to a lowered aircraft elevator. The elevator then needed to be raised to the loading decks. There were three steps from the truck to the venue before the staff team could get working.
- After transferring the pallets from the open container to the aircraft elevator, we had to wait five to 15 minutes for the elevator to reach the hangar bay and then the flight deck.
- This process could take anywhere from 45 minutes to two hours depending on the other vendors that needed to load into the venue as well.

As we started to put our plans in place for our audition, we had to work backwards, building an event timeline to figure out when to set up the kitchen, ready the firing line, and get station equipment up and spread out through the massive venue. Because we had a great understanding of our Event Lifecycle, we presented one of the best timelines for success before we even had an actual trial run.

From that point forward, we became a trusted advisor for both our clients *and* the venue, and our company became the go-to for major clients coming into San Diego. Some of our events included a 5,000-guest plated event for the Rugby Championships, a 36-station pharmaceutical convention outing on multiple levels, and a corporate picnic event including carnival booths, family games, inflatables, and, of course, BINGO!! The success and revenue growth at Midway helped with a significant increase for event awards and closings because we could use the venue as an example of how we could handle a client's event anywhere in California.

Our company went on to produce events at wineries, golf courses, museums, private beach mansions, massive horse ranch villas in the hills, concession events in multiple states, and empty fields with breathtaking views of the Pacific Ocean or San Diego Bay. We even had the chance to be one of five caterers to participate in the Guinness World Record attempt at the World's Largest BBQ in Chicago. Don't be afraid to be one of many on a venue's preferred catering list, but do figure out how to be the best company on that list.

Why Non-Exclusive Venue Relationships Work

Most off-premise caterers are reliant on their relationships with non-exclusive venues. These are venues that are not owned or managed by the caterer and often have a preferred caterers list. Unfortunately, many caterers feel beholden to these venues and do not approach them as collaborative partners in business. They actually often resent the owners and managers of the venues where they spend so much time operating. Forward-thinking caterers must change this mindset and start working on developing strong relationships with these venue representatives at all levels. The benefits of relationships at non-exclusive venues are three-fold:

- To encourage more opportunities for revenue growth (for both parties)
- To minimize challenges with onsite event production (for both parties)
- To eliminate risk and reduce expenses by being a vendor only (for the caterer)

Maximizing event potential at each non-exclusive venue and gathering a large list of non-exclusive venues only helps caterers offer myriad options to both new and existing clients.

Opportunities for Revenue Growth

Depending on your geographic location and the type of events your catering company specializes in, being on a non-exclusive venue preferred catering list and successfully working with the venue operators will increase annual revenue. The catering company must be the driving force in delivering new business development and increased revenue opportunities to the venue. The most successful non-exclusive venue caterers understand this and are creative in encouraging proactive sales opportunities by:

- Understanding the customer buying cycle
- Encouraging cross-team sales opportunities
- Upselling to customers to increase commission potential
- Creating collaborative marketing initiatives, including sponsoring networking events

Understanding the Customer Buying Cycle

Each non-exclusive venue has specific attributes and features that separate it from others. Great caterers identify these differences and invest time in understanding why customers are attracted to each and every venue. It is important to recognize the typical buying pattern of a new catering customer for their special event:

- Determining a date
- Venue selection based on date availability
- Vendor selection based on approved vendor list (caterer, florist, entertainment, etc.)

The first two steps are interchangeable depending on the customer's priorities. A corporate client may have a specific date for their employee holiday party and will select a venue strictly based on the availability of that date. On the flip side, a bride may have her heart set on one particular venue, having dreamed of holding her wedding there since she was a little girl. She will be flexible with available dates so she can have her special day at that particular venue.

In both of these situations, the venue brings the business opportunities to the vendors on the list. A great catering sales team recognizes this typical pattern and should put all business development efforts into actually making step three the *first* step their customers take. By doing this, the caterer is bringing the business to the venue and will be recognized as a proactive partner. Emphasizing this two-way approach to business development makes the caterer stand out among other competitors on the preferred list.

Encouraging Cross-Team Selling

How can you accomplish a two-way approach, or cross-team selling? By developing a proactive, company-wide venue business development strategy composed of customized plans for each non-exclusive venue. It is important to categorize your venues into various priority tiers to determine the number of initiatives within each strategy.

Caterers can establish priority tiers by encouraging sales leadership to meet with venue leadership and ask four important questions:

- What is your vision as it relates to special events?
- What are your strategic goals?
- What are your financial goals?
- What are your expectations for your preferred caterers?

Remember that events are more often than not secondary to the venue's primary mission, an extra source of income but usually *not* the venue's main purpose. Asking the questions above should provide a clearer picture of your responsibilities as the caterer and the venue's expectations of you. At the very least, they are a starting point for developing a collaborative business relationship.

Once you have the answers to these questions, both teams can work together to create a cross-team selling strategic plan to achieve the venue's and caterer's objectives.

Examples of strategic sales plan items include:

- Achieving required event revenue minimums
- Achieving specific numbers each year for each of the following:
  - New clients
  - Repeat clients
  - Catered events
- Updating website and marketing collateral pieces
- Participating in collaborative networking events (i.e., open houses)

Upselling to Customers to Increase Commission Potential and Committing to Paying Commissions

Paying commissions to the venue is a third area of revenue growth. This tends to be the biggest challenge caterers have in establishing a positive collaborative relationship with the non-exclusive venue.

It's imperative to view the commission structure as a win for both parties. The caterer typically can budget commission costs into their pricing structure. Once the event is completed, the commission should be paid in a timely manner to the venue.

If the caterer can upsell more food, beverage, equipment, or decor to the booked customer, these benefits both organizations with a larger event sale and a more enticing commission payout. The non-exclusive venue should recognize their top revenue-producing catering partners and want to continue relationships with them. Those caterers that do not produce will eventually be removed from or replaced by another catering company on the preferred vendor list.

Creating Collaborative Marketing Initiatives including Sponsorship of Networking Events

Caterers are usually asked to provide complimentary marketing initiatives on an annual basis. Examples include catering open house events, providing updated photography for the venue's website, updating venue content on their own websites, and advertising in venue collateral brochures. Investing financial resources and time in developing a mutually beneficial marketing plan should help bring in new customers as well as refresh and remind existing clients about renting the venue.

Minimize Challenges for Onsite Event Production

Once you start a partnership relationship with a venue, both companies act as an extension of the other. As the caterer begins to meet with clients, your company becomes a trusted advisor for the client. Even though your catering company doesn't own the venue, your client won't care. As their trusted advisor, your clients will expect the following:

- You have thought of everything
- You are an expert in the venue because of past experiences there
- Your entire team (operations managers, culinary leads) are able to attend onsite client meetings to walk the client through the day of execution if requested
- Your company will keep them from experiencing horror stories that they hear or read about

Over the years, our catering company had exclusive venues that we managed and non-exclusive locations where our company was one of up to 12 other companies on the preferred catering list. In order to make our company stand out and convince clients we could help them achieve their goals, we shared examples of our successes and experiences. When our sales team reached the final stages of closing the business, we scheduled a client walkthrough with the expectation that the client would make a decision after that meeting. During the walkthrough, we would share the following:

- When our truck arrives, we will unload here and park the truck over there out of sight of guests.

- Our staff will park in this location so your guests will have access to the front of the lot.
- During the event, we use this path for service and replenishment so your guests are not inconvenienced.
- Bars will have extra staff for the first hour to help with the lines. We usually like to tray pass in this area, which helps the bars as well.
- The venue does have a dumpster on site, but if it's full we will take trash back to our commissary when we finish. This will save you on any extra charges.

In several partnership relationships, our company offered our expertise to help the new venue open and market to the community. We worked with the venue to help create the standard operating procedures and the rules for operating. By assisting with these documents, our company helped design the processes for all other catering companies. Since our company was known for a high level of service and experience, the standards and operational expectations were set very high for every other vendor. Below is a short item list taken from the catering and vendor guidelines that we created for working with XYZ venue:

- Welcome to XYZ Venue! It is our goal that the following rules and guidelines will provide the necessary information for a productive, safe, and enjoyable experience during your allotted time at the aquarium. Please remember that special events are merely an extension of our normal operating hours.

- It is the responsibility of the CATERER to see that all XYZ Venue (shall be known as XYZ) rules and guidelines are followed by all catering staff working an event.
- A walk through of the facility with one of the venue's special events staff is essential for both the CATERER and the lessee, prior to each event.
- The CATERER must provide a floor plan or layout of their service prior to the event. Consideration must be given to placement of heating elements and smoke detectors. Barbecues are not allowed anywhere inside the facility.

Once you understand and establish your company's event lifecycle, building your internal processes for each venue becomes easier with each new venue. Two important steps within your event lifecycle are communication and documentation. There are three different communication layers that need to be considered when setting up your process and documentation for a new venue. These layers are:

With the venue:

- A good contract to eliminate last minute changes with the client
- A process to document your change order rules and how the process will be used
- A communication process that starts with your sales team and not with the venue. A weekly call with the venue to review upcoming events and post event analysis

Within your company:

- Schedule a pre-event call with client to confirm final guest count before your weekly Production Meeting
- Review venue contract and rules as they relate to each event
- Train sales on Change Order rules and how they will be used
- Process for human interaction when client changes are requested after the weekly Production Meeting
- A process for communicating event details to staff prior to the event
- Set up your Supervisor/Captain packets, which include the final arrangements and details

With the client:

- Schedule a pre-event call with client to confirm final guest count
- Use this pre-event call as an opportunity to review the contract and venue rules
- Educate your client on Change Order rules and how they will be used
- Ensure that your contract with the venue does not allow for the client to make last minutes changes directly with the venue

Eliminate Risk And Reduce Expenses By Being A Vendor Only

The third benefit of investing in non-exclusive relationships is minimal risk for you as the caterer from a contract perspective, either as the management company running the venue or as the actual owner of the space. This allows your leadership and management team to focus on catering as their primary business. This also should provide more time to look out for new venues opening in your region and to pay attention to the venue representatives with whom you are already working. Three specific advantages of being a vendor only with the venue include:

- Low financial investment
- Minimal operational and facility expertise
- Reduction of necessary full-time staff

Low Financial Investment

Most caterers are in the business to create and service events. Owning or operating a venue is a large financial investment without guarantees for solid bookings. An average venue hosts 60 to 70 events per year, while functioning as a 365 day per year physical operation. Sample costs to run a venue include:

- Marketing and advertising
- Building maintenance and repairs
- Overhead costs, including gas, water, electric and garbage removal
- Cleaning
- City licenses
- Kitchen maintenance and upkeep if there is a production kitchen
- Parking lot upkeep and maintenance
- Landscaping and signage
- Sales and operational staff

Minimal Operational and Facility Expertise

You can learn real estate and facility management, but these are not typically a catering company's primary focus. Instead, caterers can make suggestions for operational and facility improvements that the venue can make at their expense.

Fewer Full-Time Staffing Requirements

By working as a vendor supporting venue operation, the caterer will most likely work remotely without committing full-time, on-site staff. This reduces the caterer's payroll costs as well as human resource management.

Lastly, as one vendor on a non-exclusive venue list, it is so important to open the lines of communication and be readily available to make recommendations for improvements or changes. An annual meeting is a great way to reiterate the relationship as a business partnership. Bringing leaders from your organization, including members of your finance, sales, human resources, marketing, service, and operations departments, will show a well-rounded approach. Some examples of agenda items for these meetings include:

- Sample proposals (past and future based on exhibits)
- Number of catered events per year
- Number of site visits tracked (booked vs. showings)
- Number of new clients brought in by the catering sales team
- Annual commissions paid
- Annual revenue growth comparison from previous year

- New hires (staffing changes)
- Marketing and website updates
- Operations and service team recommendations or challenges within the facility
- Invitations to large client event tastings
- Brainstorming for future networking opportunities
- Annual comparison to other caterers' event activity

See you in the next Catering Chronicle...

There's still one more Catering Chronicle!

It All Starts Here!

Running a Great Production Meeting

Francisco Christian

Jennifer Perna

Editor - Elizabeth Heaton

Illustrator - Andy Andersen

www.cateringchronicles.com

It All Starts Here! Table of Contents

Catering Chronicles

OPERATIONS:

Our Production Meeting started out like hundreds of past meetings. We typically held them on Tuesday and looked over every event in detail for the upcoming two weeks. The salesperson was reviewing an event planned for May 7th, and we were discussing it on April 21. Food, beverage, equipment and staff all looked good.

Salesperson: "Oh yeah, one last item. I sold the client a full-sized sand volleyball court, but we are waiting on the venue to get back to us on approval."

Frank: "Wait…. but this event is in a hotel ballroom...on the third floor! Are you sure you mean *this* event?"

Salesperson: "Yep, I threw a price out there, and the client went for it. Do you think you can do it for what I charged?"

Frank: "So, you want me to work with the budget you have, figure out how to get three to four yards of sand up to the third-floor ballroom, and stake down the net, and do that all with a four-hour set up time."

Salesperson: "Yeah, that about sums it up."

Frank: "Do we get to leave the sand and let the hotel clean it up?"

Salesperson: "Oh no, we have to get it all out afterwards, and if we leave any sand anywhere in the hotel, we will be charged a huge cleaning fee that I can't pass along to the customer."

Frank (*in the quietest, calmest, and most unshaken voice I could muster)*: "Well, at least we have two weeks to make this happen."

Salesperson: *With a huge smile and getting ready to walk out of the conference room.* "Well, 11 days since it's next Saturday! Thank you. I know you and your team will figure it out."

Frank: FACEPALM!!!!!

What a whirlwind those 11 days were. We had to get a production plan, resources, vendors, SAND, equipment to load in and remove said sand from the ballroom, equipment to contain the sand, and proper weights for the net while the drinking event patrons did their best Top Gun volleyball impressions. Thankfully our warehouse and production staff were able to pull this off, and the client was blown away by the end product.

The downside? While the production team was completely focused on this single event, we had almost 50 others that needed attention during those 11 days. Production loves to create one-of-a-kind experiences, but the salesperson should have brought the operations team in as soon as they knew beach volleyball was a possibility. If our team was aware during the proposal process, we could have been more profitable, less stressed, and avoided issues with other events being produced during that time.

SALES:

I have seen a lot of salespeople, event producers, and sales assistants dread the weekly production meetings. Sometimes this dread turned to actual fear. Fear of embarrassment, ridicule, and disappointment from the operations team members. I never understood this reaction. The production meeting was the opportunity for the operations team to hear the sales team's voices. If they walked in with an open mind, accepted feedback, and looked at this weekly meeting as an opportunity to learn, it was a win in the long run. With that in mind, I spent many hours coaching my team to be prepared, organized, and invested in making the most of this valuable time with operations.

Salespeople often worried that food would run out at their events. (Why? Because salespeople always promise the customer that their event will be perfect, and running out of food is the quickest way to ruin an event. *"We have catered thousands of events. Based on our experience with food volume, you will be fine."* But there's always this niggle in the back of your mind: *"What if they eat way more than expected?!"*) The production meeting was a collaborative setting where food volume was reviewed and approved by the culinary team, our experts in food volume. Using the production meeting to get their guidance and become more practiced made food volume concerns go away.

It is always the salesperson's job to provide relevant and detailed information to make the rest of the team feel as invested in the customer relationship as she is. The operations teams could ask questions about the client and the event like, *"Have we done an event for them before?" "Is this the same person met in the tasting room?"* and *"How long has this person been our client?"* All questions about customer relationships that only get asked--and therefore information that only gets shared--in the production meeting.

The weekly meeting was the best time for salespeople to further develop camaraderie with the back of house team. It took some time, but in the long run, my anxious salespeople ultimately became better and more confident salespeople. They realized the warehouse, service, and culinary teams were the experts, and this was the forum to share their experience on how to make the event better. They made every decision together as a team based on what made sense for the company, and, ultimately, what would create an extraordinary client event experience. In the thousands of production meetings I sat in during my career, I must have said, *"What is in the best interest of the client?"* thousands of times. But this was the key: *nobody had to win in that meeting room other than the client.*

My sales team members ended up looking forward to attending production meetings, as they left each one reassured that extra care and attention went into the production of their events because they were organized and prepared to talk about it in the meeting.

PRODUCTION MEETING - IT ALL STARTS HERE

The production meeting, also called the operations meeting (OM) or banquet event order (BEO), meeting is very different from the sales meeting; they should not be confused. We will refer to this meeting as the production meeting. The priority of the production meeting is to break down all aspects of the catering or special event. By the end of the meeting, staffing, operations, culinary, and sales should have everything they need to produce the event. By taking the time to break down the event to its lowest common denominator, all departments in the business will run most efficiently.

Typically, the production meeting is held on a separate day and time from the sales meeting to allow for sharing important information from the sales meeting. In some operations, a production meeting may be on Tuesday morning immediately following the sale meeting.

In the following sections, we will discuss the purpose of the production meeting from both the sales and production vision of what needs to be accomplished. The production meeting should review events two weeks from the meeting date in detail, while also addressing any changes to events for the upcoming week. Someone from the operations team should be assigned to both take notes about event changes and then email them to the group post-meeting. This is a great check and balance and allows for training new members of your team, which in turn should produce fewer event changes as the weeks progress.

Remote Working in a Post Covid World

As we have all learned during the pandemic, remote working can be a positive for some organizations.

Well run sales and operations teams have their processes mapped and trained so that staff can work anywhere and still make information available to other departments on a timely basis, ensuring their success.

As companies return to pre-Covid revenue levels over the next few years, being flexible with employees' remote work schedules will be an advantage to keeping staff. Production meetings can be handled remotely, but you need to be a good manager and set deadlines and communicate regularly. This includes establishing effective communication processes and rules for email, video and conference calls.   Holding your employees accountable while they work from home will keep the information flowing for others to do their work and allow for training to be ongoing for your mobile workforce.

Some thoughts:

- If an account manager or event producer is attending the production meeting, the salesperson should be in the office during that time.
- Tastings should not be scheduled during the production meeting.
- It is a necessity to track packing slips and notes from the previous meeting.
- All departments are in this together: use each week as a training opportunity and not a scolding session.

SALES:

The production meeting is separate from a sales meeting. In fact, the sales meeting should be completely irrelevant to the production meeting. A sales meeting should be about future business development and strategic growth, while the production meeting should focus on the present, i.e. the next two weeks. Lastly, past events should not be discussed in production meetings.

OPERATIONS:

From the Operations point of view, the production meeting is the time to make each event successful. This is the opportunity for the salesperson, coordinator, or event producer to get all the information out of their own heads and share the full vision for the event with the team. If your organization has a full event software system to capture all the details, the production meeting offers a time to review details that may need to be added to the software.

The production meeting should be run by the director of operations, general manager, executive chef, or owner. Anyone but the sales manager. The sales manager should be focusing on generating revenue and training the sales team. The company will not want the sales manager stuck in sales meetings and production meetings during the week. The company wants the non-sales side of the business to "What If" scenario the upcoming events for the next 10 days. Typically, sales is focused on a single event or only a few events, whereas operations is focused on the cumulative events coming up in the next weeks and months. While each company tracks their event calendar differently, the basics of the production meeting are the same.

SALES:

In an ideal world, the production meeting should be a quick, snapshot review of the event paperwork, with all the important information already detailed in full. The salesperson must diligently follow consistent, company-wide rules to ensure that hot button issues are highlighted in a prominent location on the paperwork. The detailed paperwork should speak to the entire event in case all parties involved in production cannot be present at the production meeting but still know all the information.

A rule of thumb for production meeting attendance is *every person in the room must have a reason to be there.* An extensive amount of time is required, so it is important to think through a rotation of salespeople for their own events rather than asking them to sit through the entire company's two weeks of events.

Salespeople should spend their time selling. For that reason, if a salesperson has an event producer or sales assistant who handles all production elements, they should be completely capable of representing the salesperson at the production meeting. This means they need to have all the answers to potential questions from the operations team. "I don't know that answer, but I will get back to you after I talk to the salesperson" means the production meeting was a waste of time for all departments.

Since the meeting focuses on a two-week timeframe, there should be limited changes to events that week, allowing for a quick review to discuss them. Most of the meeting time should be spent on the initial discussion of an event. This is the opportunity to break down load in and out, staff needs, special circumstances at the venue, client requests, delivery timing, purchasing, etc. This allows the warehouse, culinary and service teams to organize the upcoming event needs and create cumulative purchase orders for the weeks and months to come. The further out operations know about an event, the more resource planning can be done, such as trucks, equipment, disposables, and, most importantly, human resources to successfully produce the event.

The meeting leader should keep the meeting on track and time to allow all departments to ask questions. More importantly, the meeting leader needs to be conscious of additional costs departments may be asking sales to add to the events. Once an event is confirmed and contracts have been signed, the profitability of the event, and ultimately the company, is in the hands of the operations department. Operations sometimes try to make the event easier to produce by adding additional staff, equipment, and resources whose costs often can't be passed on to the client. While some of these items may be necessary and event profitability will have to take a hit, this becomes a training opportunity for future events. We call this consistent approach to every event the company's Knowledge Management System. By creating a repeatable process for every event, the company will develop the Event Lifecycle for new employees to follow. Stay tuned to learn more about the Event Lifecycle in future Catering Chronicles.

SALES:

It is imperative to develop realistic production paperwork deadlines based on the meeting schedule and the customer contracts. Every operations team member needs to be aware of the contractual agreements established by their own company, including the additions, reductions, and substitutions policies. Once you have company-wide production paperwork deadlines in place, sales and operations must adhere to these requirements. In order to make the production meeting most effective, we recommend that you set these guidelines to allow time for the operations team to review all paperwork PRIOR to the meeting rather than in the meeting itself. Lastly, as a courtesy to the operations team, advanced paperwork is appreciated for large events. The salespeople should use their best judgement and share a copy of the proposal/contract and tentative orders with the operations team well in advance.

Here are a couple of scenarios to set up your production meeting in your organization.

CALENDAR OF PRODUCTION MEETING GUIDELINES EXAMPLE #1

Suggested Production Meeting Times and Purpose

Tuesday 8:30 AM

Discuss upcoming Friday through Sunday events

Thursday 8:30 AM

Discuss upcoming Monday through the following Thursday events

Event/Tasting Paperwork Guidelines and Deadlines

If Your Event Is:	Your Paperwork is Due:
Monday	the prior Wednesday by 12 PM
Tuesday	the prior Wednesday by 12 PM
Wednesday	the prior Wednesday by 12 PM
Thursday	the prior Wednesday by 12 PM
Friday	Monday by 4 PM
Saturday	Monday by 4 PM
Sunday	Monday by 4 PM

CALENDAR OF PRODUCTION MEETING GUIDELINES EXAMPLE #2

Suggested Production Meeting Times and Purpose

Tuesday 10 AM   Post sales meeting on the same day, discuss two weeks of events

Wednesday 8:30 AM   Standalone meeting to discuss two weeks of events

Event/Tasting Paperwork Guidelines and Deadlines

If Your Event Is: Your Paperwork is Updated:

Upcoming weekend (Thursday-Monday)

By the end of the day of the production meeting

Following Week

By the Friday after the production meeting

This schedule allows for the kitchen, warehouse, and staffing departments to handle the changes for the upcoming weekend and plan for the following week's work over the weekend when sales may not be in the office.

What should be present at a production meeting?

- Final Proposal (signed off by the client)
- Floor Plan/Set Up Map
- Production Timeline
- Vendor Load In Schedule
- Directions/Google Map
- Kitchen and Beverage Sheet
- Warehouse Packing List
- Staffing Schedule

PRODUCTION MEETING DETAILS

Now, let's get into how a production meeting should go for each event. The following areas will include specific details that need to be addressed based on the type of event, though some details apply to all events. This is not a comprehensive list, but it gives your team a template to create their own priorities based on the type of events.

The first time an event is reviewed in the production meeting, sales should be reading from what the client has in their hands. Operations should be comparing what sales is reading to the reports they use to execute the event (i.e., warehouse packing list, food kitchen sheet or schedule). During the second week an event is reviewed, the assumption is that sales made the necessary changes. At that point you would only be focusing on hot button items. This will help with meeting time efficiency.

1. Proposal/Contract Details

All Event Types

- Payments and signed contracts received
- Food leave time and any additional leave times for events with multiple trucks
- Start and end times match on packing lists and staffing sheets
    - Event times vs food times
    - Bar times
- Load in/load out and any event planner production schedules
- Event hot button issues that the salesperson discussed with customer
- How many kitchens onsite
- Group demographics
- Event history (with us vs. other catering companies)
- Power locations
- Trash onsite or return to office
- Water disposal onsite

2. Menu Page/Packing List Details

All Event Types

- Recipe descriptions - client document matches kitchen production sheet including additions, omissions, and substitutions
- Kitchen production sheet lists all the correct ingredients
- Item quantities verified based on tray passed, buffet, station or plated presentations
- On site prep and equipment needs review

- Food issues related to hold time
- Stage of prep when recipes leave the warehouse kitchen
- Photos of items as they should look to remove interpretation on site
- Modifications to recipes requested during client tasting
- Any late food deliveries needed for this menu

Concession/Public Sales

- Dry ice for site storage
- Case counts match sales projections
- Produce cut on site or pre-cut deliveries
- Condiment dispensers

Family Style

- Portions will work with size of platters and dishes chosen
- Garnish
- Portioned in pans at kitchen
- Onsite cooking instructions

Passed HD

- Food volume
- Kitchen space

Picnic/Casual

- Food issues related to hold times for hot food cooked and finished on site
- Correct salad or dessert choices when menus offer choices

Seated/Plated

- Diagrams or photos of finished plates
- Estimated timing of entire plate up
- Staff meals and ready time
- Late deliveries of hot food if set up is complicated
- Number of kitchens needed based on floor plan/venue space

Station Buffet

- Special layouts or diagrams based on decor that might hinder the cooking area
- Health or state required equipment that might change the way the recipe is produced
- Number of buffets, access points, and design (i.e., double sided or station attended)

3. Beverage Page/Packing List Questions

General Details

- How many bars/points of service and standard setup
  - Number of bartenders (i.e., how many kits/vermouths do I really need to send)
- Type of product (Beer/Wine/Soda or Full Bar)
- Brands of offerings the same as packages sold
- Menu signs for bars
- Ice needs
- Rentals or specialty bars other than tables and risers
- Substitutions charged for accordingly
- Any special toast and timing

- Batch at Kitchen or onsite
- Mixologist on site
- Process for making beverage runs to shop or store
  - Who makes a run one is needed?
  - Client approval for price increase
- Specific drinks for VIPs

Self Service

- Proper serving vessels for the type of drink
- Ice chest, beverage barrels, or larger ice tubs to hold enough product
- Location for re-icing
- Refreshing and removal of water from ice tubs

Hosted

- Donated product and any license issues
- Drink tickets
- Any consumption information needed for approved service
- Specialty choices if packages are sold
- Beer gardens, permits, or keg related issues if you are doing draft/canned beer offerings
- Correct choices if menu includes beverage options
- Ice quantities based on time of year and number of buffets

Cash Bar

- Pricing for registers or digital platform
- Cash banks
- Inventory sheets
- Over ring sheets
- Onsite cash room/security detail if needed

4. Equipment Packing List

General

- Delivered to site (if outsourced)
- Set up by outsourced company
    - What time onsite
    - Which of your team members is managing?
    - Pickup time
    - Final floor plan/diagram sent
    - Outsourced company contact/lead manager name and contact number
    - After 5/back line phone number listed for last minute runs
- Back of house supply kits (event and culinary)
- Special notes converted into items if using software
- Inventory overbooking
- Provided by venue
    - Specify equipment
    - Name of the Onsite Venue Manager
    - Clear definition of who is setting up the onsite equipment
        - If the equipment is setup by venue, define set up times

Concessions

- Hand wash stations
- Additional propane

Family Style

- Platters and serving utensils
- Menu cards

- Determine the volume of food ratio and if providing overage

Full Seated Buffet

- Kitchen equipment for finishing onsite

Picnic/Casual

- Number of buffets/grills/points of service
- Equipment needs match the menu
- Additional set up time or warehouse staff needed for larger items

Seated/Plated

- Number of plating lines and equipment to match
- Plating line diagram to double check equipment packing lists
- Proper holding equipment for hot food and cold courses
- Ovens and proper truck scheduling
- Lighting, tenting, and power for plating area/ tent
- "Building" kitchen space (i.e., movable walls/ pipe and drape)
- Specialty cakes or desserts that need to be safely packed
- Gifts dropped to the warehouse from the client

Station Buffet

- Proper handling material needed to get equipment across the venue location
- Station equipment packages labeled properly

- Station diagrams/pictures for staff to set up their stations on their own

5. Staff Schedule

- Supervisor and chef start times are early enough to check truck and culinary before leaving for event
- Number of staff match the proposal to the staffing sheet
- Mix of seasoned and training staff
- Any special staff needs for the client or wedding planner
- Proper number of runners, station attendants, station chefs
- Timing to unload, set and tear down station at the end of the event
- Scullery, set up staff, and runners from kitchen to the plating line
- Determine what positions can double up during plate-up

6. Miscellaneous and Vendor Information

- Power needs
- Delivery time
- Flowers or centerpieces
- Pick up times same day or any equipment returning to the office
- Meals for vendors that remain on site
- Vendor break rooms if contracted
- Schedule for loading area prior to and after event
- Specific onsite staging areas if required
- Onsite contact names and cell phone numbers for each vendor representative

- Attach copies of vendor contracts (remove $ $ page) for captain's paperwork

Production Deadlines Prior to the Meeting

Here is a list of tasks that should be completed prior to each week's production meeting:

1. Sales confirms event if it is scheduled for that week
2. Operations has all tasks related to new items or questions from the previous week's meeting
3. Sales finalizes all kitchen and staff sheets
4. Operations double checks for changes to the events coming up in the next five days. These events should be in a completion stage or even being staged and pulled in operations.

POST PRODUCTION MEETING

Once the production meeting has concluded for the week, these are the post-meeting action items:

1. The notes from the meeting are emailed to sales, operations, culinary, and staffing, as well as any other managers who request the information. By keeping track of notes and required changes on a weekly basis, managers can understand who needs more training or support. Include deadlines for changes. Remember, this is a tool for the business and should not be used as a place to call out mistakes.

2. Sales will have all their changes completed either by the end of the business day or by the time the kitchen comes back in the morning. This gives operations a chance to plan for the rest of the week with the most up to date information. Managing the customers is very important. You should share key dates and timing with customers so that they know when the event must be completely final with no changes to ensure the event's success.
3. The sales team should email operations when their part of the task list is completed. This helps with accountability and allows operations to move the event through the production process. The production meeting manager should communicate changes to the sales manager to make sure they are addressed in a timely way.
4. If there are changes to the event after the final production meeting, these should be conveyed in a call or in-person meeting with the department affected by the changes. An email with the approved changes should be sent from the sales team to the department so they have a hard copy of the requested changes.

REMEMBER!

Operations is the last line of defense for every event that sales confirm. While there is always the competitive nature of sales versus operations, the golden rule in operations is "Ours is to ask and not assume." After personally sitting through or running production meetings for more than 10,000 events, I can tell you that following the same line of questioning for each event is the way to be successful.

Whether the party is for 10 people or 50,000, the basic needs are the same from an operations standpoint. Every dollar that sales bring into the event starts out with a very finite gross profit that the company counts on. The operations team goal is to not let pennies and nickels slip away; they accomplish this by watching all angles of an event. For example, let's say the warehouse team is trying to keep overtime costs down for a particularly busy time of year. If the warehouse doesn't know that sales is expecting three or four staff members to help with setup and tear down of an event until the week of the production meeting, labor costs may go into overtime or double time. This oversight, not covered in the production meeting, will cost the company money that may or may not be passed along to the customer.

Another example is renting trucks during the holiday season. Usually, the warehouse has to place an order month in advance to compete with other delivery companies, which boost their fleets during these times. If the truck count changes the week of the event, the warehouse may not be able to secure extra vehicles. Worse than that, there might be a truck available, but it could take a few staff members an extra 30 to 45 minutes to go pick up the truck on Friday after three PM. Usually this is when you need the staff on site to work on events for that night or tomorrow. It's also often the busiest travel time on the road.   Planning ahead can prevent all these costly challenges.

Culinary needs to know the week prior so they can start purchasing and securing items from their vendors. If there is a change to the menu or recipe substitutions that the kitchen is not aware of, they might have to secure the new items for more money at a retail location. Even more costly is an item that has to be delivered from the vendor the day of the event. This throws off production timing and leaves a huge window of error if there are further issues that day. This could lead to a customer complaint because that is the only item that the customer cares about. Another concern is that the onsite staff may not finish the preparation, and then someone from the kitchen staff has to swing by the event to ensure execution. All of these add to costs and contribute to dimes and pennies disappearing along the way.

See you in the next Catering Chronicle...

NOTES, THOUGHTS AND NEXT STEPS

Made in the USA
Monee, IL
12 July 2021

73408122R10059